FANBOYS: Poems about Teaching and Learning

poems by

Lani T. Montreal

Finishing Line Press
Georgetown, Kentucky

FANBOYS
Poems about Teaching and Learning

Copyright © 2018 by Lani T. Montreal
ISBN 978-1-63534-728-9 First Edition
All rights reserved under International and Pan-American Copyright Conventions.
No part of this book may be reproduced in any manner whatsoever without written permission from the publisher, except in the case of brief quotations embodied in critical articles and reviews.

ACKNOWLEDGMENTS

This project, initially titled *Faculty Development*, began over six years ago, or perhaps it is always beginning. I would get epiphanies of verse every now and then, in between grading papers and making school lunches, but the demands of motherhood and a full-time job became ever more overwhelming, and creative endeavors were set aside. In 2015, I was lucky enough to receive the Djerassi Resident Artist Program Award through the 3Arts Program, and so I immediately applied for a sabbatical from work. I have been working full-time at Malcolm X, one of the City Colleges of Chicago, for seven years and this would be an awesome break, right? Well, a month before my sabbatical started, I was diagnosed with early stage breast cancer. Ductal Carcinoma in Situ (DCIS), my doctor said over the phone, as I was paying for back-to-school stuff at Marshall's, my 10-year-old daughter in tow. I cried, of course, not knowing what it entailed, as I gave my credit card to the cashier. (God forbid something so dire interrupted shopping.) Since then, I have had a lumpectomy, radiation therapy, and have been taking the once-a-day breast cancer pill to prevent recurrence. My awesome caregivers, apprised of the importance of this artist residency program, made sure I was right on schedule. And true enough, Djerassi proved to be the most consoling treatment regimen of all. While there, I tried writing a poem a day, which was actually more challenging than I thought, especially when recovering from treatment trauma. Nevertheless, the breathtaking redwood trees, good food, and new-found friends made it a propitious time for verse and rhythm to play on paper. Of course, without the support of my beloved partner, Luis Bermudez, our beautiful children, Cameron and Alexa, and my vixious posse of Albany Park, Chicago women, this chapbook would have languished in perpetua. I'm also grateful to my Toronto BFF Melanya Liwanag-Aguila, who illustrated my cover, and to my former MFA professor, now my colleague, Ivor Irwin, for helping me edit and revise the poems. This chapbook, FANBOYS, is dedicated to my precious family, both biological and chosen, my colleagues and students at MXC, and most importantly, my mother, Mely Tagasa. Thank you for teaching me how to learn.

Publisher: Leah Maines
Editor: Christen Kincaid
Cover Art: Melanya Liwanag-Aguila
Author Photo: Djerassi Resident Artists Program
Cover Design: Elizabeth Maines McCleavy

Printed in the USA on acid-free paper.
Order online: www.finishinglinepress.com
also available on amazon.com

Author inquiries and mail orders:
Finishing Line Press
P. O. Box 1626
Georgetown, Kentucky 40324
U. S. A.

Table of Contents

- Andragogy 1
- Pedagogy 2
- Tenure 3
- Habit of mind 4
- Student Success 5
- Placement 6
- Time Management 7
- Exit Portfolio 9
- Calibration 10
- Faculty Development 12
- Adjunct 13
- The Essay You Asked For 14
- Framework: On the occasion of a hate crime committed at an art school and the response that came after 15
- Rubric 16
- Residency 17
- Parts of Speech: A Love Poem 18
- Snow Days 19
- Listening to Mary 20
- Scientific Inquiry: A Villanelle 21
- Fellowship: A Pantoum 22
- Howling at Djerassi 23
- Elegy for Resilient Skin 24
- Sans Rhyme 25
- La Suegra 26
- A Ghazal for Oh Daddy Oh 27
- An Elegy for Part of Me 29
- Afterthought 30
- Missing Gems 31
- Gendered Relations 32
- Rhetoric 35

Andragogy

The smell of shit stays in your hand
even after six washings; this you conclude
as you scoot to a panel on assessing
learning; stressing, cursing, fingerfood-forking
as if there is something more bruising
than toilet training or the traumatic dropping
of fecal matter on clean, size 3T underwear.

You learn.

Pedagogy

She cries,
her mommy stuck in her throat
in the pit of her stomach
in the twitch of her little hips
in the cross of her eyes;
she cries,
over pain that is now
here.

"It hurts."
Where baby?
"Nowhere."
"It hurts."
Point for me.
"I don't know."

She flinches,
every touch
every sound
every feeling;
she senses
your truth
in the wave of your hand
in the sweat on your forehead
in the curve of your smile

She learns.

Tenure

Hold me, dear, please hold me
The corridors are lit by fluorescent
That makes our faces look haggard
And our clothes unwashed;

I don't want to meld with the brick walls
Where no bright flier would stick
So please keep me close and hold me
Here, where my ABCs Fail me

And D is the letter of possibility
Here, where the tardies turn
The clock backwards and absences
Don't mean you are not loved

I hang on to promises of a new day
Un-watered by tears, undisturbed by life
I hang on to hurried walks in the hallways
After a missed quiz, or two days of no-show

I want to stay but will I be held
Tenderly and without discomfort?
Will my midnight sojourn into
Unmappable minds lead me
                        to everlasting bounty?

Habit of mind

What habits does our mind learn
At the ornate dining table
burdened with mama's cooking?

To not speak unless spoken to
That tyranny is acceptable
When tempered with benevolence

To not speak unless properly
That Aunt Fely is wrong to leave her home
Even when there is no comfort

To not speak unless with praise
For the dictator on the TV
Telling us to not litter or loiter after dark.

In school, we pray the angelus,
Sing the New Society song,
Listen to the sisters' quiet chatter

As they glide immaculate, pure
Bleached and treated with cornstarch;
While we soil our blues and whites

From unbridled play at recess,
Wrestling in the playground,
Flesh quivering, panties showing

What habits does our mind learn
When the tears dry and the welts heal?
To not dream, unless asleep

Student Success

In between dips of spoon in mediocre dessert,
I tell him I doubt the wisdom of giving Tara a B at midterm

The apple crumble is sweet, too sweet, the swirls of
caramel, an apology for the haphazard

sprinkling of nutmeg mix. I am grateful for the man
sitting across from me, criss-crossing stainless steel teaspoons,

ever so thoughtful about not taking more. In the
theater, I raise the armrest-cupholder, lean my limp

body, tired from multi-tasking. We finger-lock
instinctively, steal kisses through the previews, and then

Perseus is born, by water into boat. Half god,
half man, he is Paris Hilton; no need for credits

for transfer to a four-year college, no having to
assemble the parts of speech, no simplifying algebraic

expressions. With charm and divine guidance he
challenged a god; tricked into believing this is

what he wanted. He wins the battle, the girl, the trust
fund. I go home with the man; Tara waits for her grade.

Placement

When a child comes
to you, you are mistaken to
think you have a choice; he
has chosen you, the way kitty cats
rub their noses against your face
to leave a scent that says,
"You are mine."
The way
your heart sinks
at the sight of a beloved, or swoons
over scents that remind you of holidays past:
pine, roasted poultry, sugar baking in the oven,
gunpowder, crispy paper bills. You are arrogant, even
cruel, to think, "Yes, this one, and not that, pretty please
with icing on top." No, this is not so. A child comes and that is that.
        Your   livesarelinkedfromthemomenthe   grabs
  Y o u r   finger, walks with you with tentative   s t e p s
to make known his presence,
indelibly mark floors and ceilings
with his being there, forever
altering time, and space, and dinner
plans. You do not watch and wait to see
if this works, like some Christmas present
you immediately deemed "for re-gifting." He
does not come with a gift receipt; no certificate
    of authenticity or   two-year warranty;
   just a yellow carbon   copy of a transfer form,
  a Husky garbage bag   of clothes and sundry—
   a favorite action toy,   shoes that are two
    sizes bigger, and   yes, possibilities,
and confusion,   and night terrors.

Time Management

She looks at me, crystal-eyed
She is Jodie Foster post Panic Room
calm voice, stoic face
"So what is time to you?"
"How do you feel about time?"
In my mind I think about
the million and one things I could do
with my time that do not include
talking about time, but I say
Time
is never enough
is not within my control
And we let time pass
between us
the silent pauses like change
falling through pocket holes
lost in the seams
ghostly jingles.

And I take my time
because it seems I can
and wonder if I could be so brave as
to book a flight on Orbitz
fill in to and from airport codes
dates and times of arrival,
departure, while cells multiply
and synapses fail, loving spouse
in a circle of strangers, bound
by truncated calendars

And I take my time
look out the fancy glass walls from
the fifth floor with no washroom
cars passing, pedestrians crossing
purple post-its waiting for my

Three Big Things. "This is the beginning
of taking control," she says
as she waits...

And I take my time
(Homework detention again)
And I take my time
(They took the tubes out and she breathed her last)
And I take my time
(Is it really necessary for subjects and verbs to agree?)
And I take my time
(No more post-therapy hair loss)

And I take my time—
Until, I suppose, time takes me.

(Published by *Wax Poetry, Weekly Poems*, Editor's Choice 2014)

Exit Portfolio

One day I think I will keel over and die
over a stack of college essays
waiting to be scored;
it will be death by grammar
purple ink bleeding all over
the page, where I had stabbed it
to indicate a missing punctuation.

When it does happen, will it be worth it?
To care so much about a language evolving?
Devolving? Becoming a mutt? Something
hybrid? An indefinable mesh
of letters and numbers
nuf 2 ft 3" scrns stuck
2 nmbl phalanges?

Will it be worth 100-page
dissertations, written with
perfect grammar,
arguing the subversive
use of vernacular
as a way to accommodate
marginalized groups, systematically
excluded from academic discourse
that ponder their exclusion?

And when I die,
    pray
        tell

Will my elegy be proofread?

(Published online by the National Council of Teachers of English of
English/Two-Year College English Association for National Poetry Month
Celebration-2011)

Calibration

Thursday at 2, we sit in chairs
still warm from quiet fidgeting;
before us: gel pens, scoring sheets,
photocopied essays from semesters past,
names crossed out as if to be revised; one
makes me wonder… is it Tasha's
from the previous fall? The swish
of the caps and the loops of the l's
seem familiar; she, with the pretty
Tweety bird eyes, always sitting in the back,
making herself small.

I remember she wrote about how
when she was four, her father
shot her mother before shooting
himself with a 45-caliber and how
she had stayed in her aunt's house
waiting
and waiting
for them to come get her
"(D)id they forget about me?" she wrote,
and then how I was at a loss about how
to respond or to score… "Tasha, good job
with your grammar—subject verb agreement, absence
of run-ons—but I am a little confused,
did you actually see the shooting?
Because if you did, it's not very clear;
what happened when you realized,
they were never coming back?"

Coherence is, after all, what we score
when we meet
to calibrate, norm,
find a reasonable range,
re-grade old papers,
make sure an A is an A and a C is a C;

"We need to be certain, you see,
if a student is indeed ready
to move on.

"We need to be calibrated."

Of course.

It is past four in January, an orange dusk
darkening, and the writing is looking
more ragged and painful
to read.

(Published online by National Council of Teachers of English of English/Two-Year College English Association for National Poetry Month Celebration 2013)
(Published by *Garland Literary Journal,* 2016)

Faculty Development

And when one faculty is developed,
what happens to the rest? Do they whither

and crack like dry hay, turn into tumble-
weeds, quietly roll in the wind, cross paths

with ghosts of cowboys killed in shoot-outs or
accidentally hit in militant

merrymaking, when random folk shoot their
guns in the air as if bullets don't fall

fast and fatally upon reveling
heads? Do they turn sour like *pansit*, left

too long out on the buffet table, then
taken to work the next day, egg noodles

mushy and stinky with yesterday's un-
fulfilled wish?

                       Or do they simply take off?

Adjunct

Not a phantom limb.

The Essay You Asked For
      (inspired by Larry Levis's "The Poem You Asked For")

My essay can't make it today
It is stuck in the snow
Its grandma just died
It has no babysitter
It was called to work
Its brother got shot,
left bleeding in the pavement
a mistaken identity
and so my essay
is grieving
is unresponsive
is stuck in the snow
It forgot its thesis
Didn't think it needed one
There's no reasoning with my essay
"Shape up or ship out," I said
but it is impermeable to threats,
only shrugged its shoulders
gave me the finger
and walked away
ML-what?!@! it screamed
Fist poised for a punch,
when I talked about format
My essay is not ready
It is insecure
It has performance anxiety
It wants a second chance
It only cares about what you think,
Yet you can't see past its imperfection.

Framework: On the occasion of a hate crime committed at an art school and the response that came after

I am silenced by your eloquence
The way you use words like utensils
spooning abstraction into my mouth
Salted, sweetened, condiments like explosives

Will you lick the drool
Drip dripping down my chin?
Will you scoop the glaze of awe
In my eyes? And use it please,
Use it to baste your tasty oration

Yum.

"We are all victims, perpetrators and witness…"
We are the whip-lashers and the whipped backs
The noose weavers and the cracked necks
The haters and the hated.

It's all good, all good, but there must be someone
Who makes all the moolah from this melee
And none I know are in this room

So please, teacher, tell me,
Deconstruct it for me and dismantle
This theoretical thing-a-ma-jig you have
Works so well to keep my tongue tied
And my balled fist to my side
So tell me, please, tell me.

Oh, you have dessert coming? Really?

Yum.

Rubric
    (For Dad)

Heart attacks come at the most inopportune times
And when it does, there is no rubric
to measure it against
Will he pass?
Will he fail?
Will he survive the monotony
of a life spent outside a studio set?
No special effects to mask
brittling bones
bungling lines spat from the side
of unparalized mouth
No CGI to animate a lifeless arm
that once cradled fantasy uzis
Samurai swords
make-believe lovers
a long-necked bottle of Tanduay rhum
my mother's strong back
my lithe 3-year-old frame
tired from play.

Residency

can't seem to write a poem
when in the company of true poets
those for whom words come
in epiphanies of light and laughter,
an ache in some undisclosed body part
in the underside of leaves,
a particular purple, the annoying whir
of mosquitoes, the distant wailing of sirens
that somehow transforms into a wolf's bay,
broken hearted, in search of a mate

I am jealous of them, these true poets
I am in awe, drawn to them like dry hay
to brushfire: willing kindling.

Parts of Speech: A Love Poem

Sometimes, there are no words for how I feel
about you, and I wonder if perhaps languages
were birthed this way; that maybe primeval
humans, frustrated with the inadequacy of gestures,
were forced to utter sounds, except they still could
not find full expression for their affection, and

so they gurgled, formed babel with the shape
of their chops, smacked tongues against teeth,
'til words woke, yet they still fell short; so they
spat nouns, forged verbs, split infinitives; strung
'em together with, yes—FANBOYS—witnessed
this lei of locution, thought wow, what strange,
what newfangled beauty, prized poultry awarded
to the finest declaimer;

after all that, the meanings misplaced
in all the wasteful interjections, they forgot
what it was that they had wanted to say;

oh well, it's okay, it's alright, it's cool, cool, cool,
'cuz now they have this thing, this wondrous
thing called language, and I bet it must be like
inventing the pen, the typewriter,
the telephone, or the internet; how someone
fell in love or ached to connect
doing something other than grunt or grab
body parts to communicate intent—
raw, abundant, resisting containment.

This, I know.

I like being silent with you. I like when we binge
on Netflix late at night, faces half-lit
by the Samsung tablet. I like not having
to say a word, yet know exactly when it's okay

to grab your crotch and make you grunt.

Snow Days

White lies
upon Chitown
but only certain hoods
are plowed, and black ice melts unseen.
Snow day

Listening to Mary

There's a hint of orange in my piece of sky,
morning, as I listen to Mary Oliver, On Being. "Soul
has become a lazy word," she says, while
my Nightsky app beeps "Tonight is clear
for stargazing." The orange disperses, diffuses
above the distant sea. A pair of kestrels glides over
the hills in frolic. The juncos chatter on
the wicker chair by the screen door. A brown stallion
with white hooves grazes on grass that
seems greener from two days of rain. "The poems
just keep coming," she says. I love Mary's voice; she
sounds like an old friend. Not old like she's 80
although that she is, promoting her latest
book of poetry at that, but old like
someone I knew in the past, but with whom I am
not intimate. In fact, she's like a woman I chatted
with at the park while babysitting or at a conference
sitting alone at a round banquet table. We hit it
off telling stories about children and health
issues, "It's downhill after 60," she says.
"Are you sure not 50? 'Cause I'm feeling it now."
We laugh, she hushes me when a speaker is on the podium;
we agree to hang out again some time, exchange
emails, maybe even numbers, but never do.

Scientific Inquiry: A Villanelle

For what is science but magic unveiled
A savant unleashed by trauma in the brain
Don't fret the banal because love will prevail

We put faith in doctors when our bodies bail
Mammograms, blood tests, emoticons for pain
For what is science but magic unveiled

I never thought of my parents as human and frail
They were magical beings and completely sane
Suffer the banal because love will prevail

An assay of America's racial travail
Reveals that there exists a deep psychic pain
For what is science but magic unveiled

That her son comes home safe is a mother's wail
Where suicide by cop is a common refrain
Don't fret the banal because love will prevail

If I know how it works, is the magic derailed?
Is the spark gone when dirty dishes remain?
For what is science but magic unveiled
Don't fret the banal because love will prevail

Fellowship: A Pantoum

The ghost stepped out from the hollow of a tree
As I walked leisurely in the wooded trail
And I didn't know whether to scream or flee
There was no mention of this in Anza's email

As I walked leisurely in the wooded trail
I remember being warned: bobcats, snakes, a mountain lion
But there was no mention of this in Anza's email
No waylaying by a tree-dwelling, ghostly scion

I remember being warned: bobcats, snakes, a mountain lion
But the wraith was quite comely, not a brute predator
No waylaying by a tree-dwelling, ghostly scion
Not today, in fact, I think I'd seen her before

The wraith was quite comely, not a brute predator
She just wanted to converse; thank god, she's not a succubus
Not today, in fact, I think I'd seen her before
In the big house, where they grow an array of cactus

She just wanted to converse; thank god, she's not a succubus
Stuck in a space so narrow, she'd been wanting to go
In the big house, where they grow an array of cactus
But she looks after the redwood, a dilemma, I know!

Stuck in a space so narrow, she'd been wanting to go
"So unfair I can't leave; why does it have to be me?"
She looks after the redwood, a dilemma I know
The ghost stepped out from the hollow of a tree.

Howling at Djerassi

The wind howls in my pod and I take a puff, then
another, 'cause it seems to want something I don't
really know what; sometimes it brings its friends along,
vroom vroom vrooming through the breaches
in the walls. Maybe they're motorcyclists
racing down the road to Alice's, maybe they're
micro tornadoes from the '70s, or maybe just more wind,
trapped in between the pods, trying to find the hills.
I try to tell my neighbor but she doesn't seem to believe.
"I don't hear anything," she says and goes back
to her reading. I told Paul, I'll try and catch it
at night when it's loudest; maybe you can help
me figure out what it wants. Well, it was loud last night.

I wanted to go outside with my top off and yell:
"See my burns, my blisters, and bumps?! See my scar
where a heated little knife sliced a piece of me last month?!?"
I'd howl at the wind, at the moon, at Mars,
at Capricornus and Deneb. See, I can take pain
any time; it reminds me that I survived, but I
can't let the wind take my breath away.

Elegy for Resilient Skin

I hold on like boa to prey,
squeezing life 'til its eyes pop
its spine breaks, its skin bruises
purple and blue; breath escaping
into nightly sighs that fog
the bathroom mirror, punctuate
what is unspoken.

I hold on like red sunset henna
staining white ceramic tiles,
my hair wrapped in smells
of earth packed in clay jars,
preserving decay, tingeing
my black and white dreams
with an orange grief.

But it
      slips,
slips,
    slips,
              slivers
                  of
           epidermis
whirlpooling like casualty
into the drain. Father's
little hand digs trenches
over once familiar territory;
and what's left in my hands
are molted memories
and over-the-counter salves
that promise density
in two weeks, tops.

(Published by *Lantern Literary Journal* 1999)

Sans Rhyme

There are things I cannot write about
Things I've seen
That resist metaphor
Irony lost in rage
In unwanted caresses
Things that defy definition
Meanings splattered in red
Red dark as first menses
Red dark as blood bathed in shadows
These are the things
I cannot pen into poetry
Things that do not have rhythm
Nor form that sway to soft air in the night
I have seen these things
In half-remembered moments
They swoop down on me
Like birds of prey
Snatching words from my mouth
before they could escape
Wrestling reason to the ground
with hard punches and jabs
before crushing
Powerful claws digging into flesh

The body of reason lies shriveled and torn
It bleeds in my mind
Like the scream that obliterates thought
The scream that is held captive
These things I cannot write about
Because they hurt
Because they come in the night
And steal me from the lap of sleep

(Published by Woman Made Gallery 2000)

La Suegra
>   *(For Bertha)*

you and I were transplanted here, cut
at the stem and soaked in water until
we grew fragile roots, thin like capillaries

that transport blood and memory from
vital organ to vital organ
we trade food like long-kept secrets, illicit

with flavor that blaspheme our mundane
expatriate existence; we speak the tongues
of our colonizers, strain our necks to

catch words between us like butterflies
in a meadow of aluminum pots
and linoleum countertops; your wooden

spoon and fork painted with generic flowers
stark against the white walls are smaller
than my mother's, but they bring me home

the way your empanadas crumble in my
mouth, your cesina like tapa
we dip in vinegar and garlic and

your bacalao becomes the story my
grandfather used to tell when he dropped salty
dried fish into a pot of boiling water

saying it was the worn sole of his favorite shoe.

(Published by *Sunday Inquirer Magazine*, Manila, Philippines 2006)

A Ghazal for Oh Daddy Oh

Never once wrote you a poem, Oh Daddy-o
You with a voice, smooth as chrome, Oh Daddy-o

Your star did froth a lethargic little foam and I wonder
If it's true you're finally home, Oh Daddy-o

No longer in the back room smelling of day-old laundry.
No, not in someone's dark and dingy dorm, Oh Daddy-o

I remember making trips at dawn to the wet market
Your kinky hair pomaded, slickly combed, Daddy-o

Flirting flawlessly with the seafood girl, you haggle
for milk fish, oyster or abalone, Daddy-o

Minced pig's lungs cooked in vinegar sauce, gambas al ajillo
Mmmm. You rocked the pan with aplomb, go Daddy go

The kitchen your kingdom, the rice cooker your right hand man
but bless your restless soul, nothing could make you not roam, Oh Daddy-o

Not a new stainless steel La Germania stove, or a spanking trove of
cast-iron cookware. No, none could keep you home, Oh Daddy-o

That time you left on Christmas eve after abusing the aperitif
Returned New Year's eve, predictable as a palindrome, woe Daddy woe

Did you think she would take you back again?
Did you think to your charms she would succumb? Aw Daddy aw

Well, it's been a while and there is no coming back
Not this time, no, gone the belligerent dome, Oh Daddy-o

Years later, back together, she groceried, a bounty from Pure Gold.
The sack of rice, 25 pounds, you carried with no groan, Oh Daddy-o

Perhaps you thought chivalry would earn her forgiveness?
Instead, a thrombosis!! In her arms you fell; gone Daddy gone

On your deathbed, prayers she intoned, then whispered, "*Mahal pa rin kita*"
And with that, you breathed your last, a sacred om Daddy om

And here I am, Lani, eldest daughter, humble storyteller, with the gall
to write a ghazal; sadly, a posthumous poem for Oh Daddy-o

(Published by *Wax Poetry, Weekly Poem* 2015)

An Elegy for Part of Me

Today is a day for grieving; for wet eyes
and tight chest, for sad songs and rain.

There's a map on my left breast where
there used to be skin, deep dark brown earth

upon which a flower has bloomed;
beside it are three imprints of an animal paw

and a horizon lines the scar
through which part of me was taken.

Afterthought

The hurts were gathered on a pile of kindling at the barn
There, where Tom clears the trail for ghosts in the winter.

There was hurt for Uncle Midas whose touch of gold kept
his loved-ones at bay. There was hurt for Medusa, whose

deathly gaze steeped in a deep well of pain. There was
hurt for the black bodies hung in the branches of poplars

and hurt for the ones suiciding in the streets of Chicago.
The hurt almost escaped when it was brought out to air,

but the flickering lights coaxed it to come down. The fire
burned high and the embers remained. The spirits consoled

and the bunnies dreamed in blue. The whales, too,
became mermen, tired of bleeding oil for lamps and butter

I guess that's what happens when hurts fester. They sing a song
to lure sailors to crash against the rocks; too vain to realize

                                                it was a dirge.

Missing Gems
(For Tionda and Diamond Bradley, missing since 2001)

There are no small brown boxes
to hold no small brown bodies, nothing
to mourn, but the passing of day into night
as she sets the table for five, but
        tucks to bed only two.

There are no small brown boxes
save for one that held their smiles;
an open-lid viewing might have
made more sense than this—a ritual
        grieving for evanescing stills.

(Published in *Mother Tongues* published by Literary Exchange, Chicago, 2003)

Gendered Relations

We are queer.
Not in the way
Queer as Folk is or
Queer Eye for the Straight Guy.
We have
unconventional friendship
you and I, taking risks
but not in the way
Will and Grace do
playing up gay-straight
sexual tension on
primetime TV.
We trade secrets
when we're drunk on chianti
in between reruns of classics
on cable TV, the boundary
between us like
unwanted ads selling
gas pain relievers
during scene breaks in
Citizen Kane, color
intruding into black and white
but not making gray areas
any clearer.

We meet in brightly lit
street corners,
you and I, gender-
bending, but not in the way
straight actors who play
transsexuals do, leaving
normal by sequence 32. We
make gender our science
experiment growing it in controlled
biospheres or leaving it to
rot and fester in dark
chemistry lab cabinets.

You say there is no
absolute truth,

waxing philosophic midway
through Symphony No. 40
In G Minor. And I,
uninspired, wonder:
If you're right then
what makes a lie a lie?
Whose truth matters when
a woman's body remembers
what her child-mind had
chosen to forget? When gender
is nothing but a prison sentence
and the judge is always
a brother of yours?

We are queer this way,
you and I, challenging
perceptions, but not like
Angelina Jolie tongueing
her handsome sib at the Oscar's.
Although it does make me curious
when I let myself dream
on nights when you call
past midnight, bold
with inebriation, and tell me you
love me, or when you
wrap my wet hands in the kitchen
towel, gently turning, like
uncooked spring rolls, our
indiscretion illumined by the
light from the half-open fridge,
or when you knead my tired feet after
a long walk on the littered sidewalks
of Chicago, when you would not even
give me a full hug, afraid perhaps
of what it might arouse? Or fearing
emasculation from a show of
unbridled affection?

It makes me quiver and smile
conjuring cinematic scenes.

No, not those my mother dreamed
for me even after the discovery of
my
woman
lover
in the closet. My fantasy
does not lead to church ceremonies
or white picket fences. It comes
with no strings attached, like
Gina Gershon molting sexuality
past the rising credits like a
disoriented boa.

We are queer this way
you and I, like
low-rise jeans snug around
my hips but letting my
ab flab hang and breathe, like
tight-ribbed designer sweater
hugging your newly-toned pecs, we
are queer this way, you and I,
and in my dreams
we make babies
born
without
umbilical cords.

(Published in *MiPoesias*, 2007)

Rhetoric
(For Mom)

This is not your hand;
This bloated fish in my latex-gloved hand,
hematomaed like the drowned corpse I saw
when I wrote about night hawks who
forage after 12 for decaying remains,
blood-debt killings, a small ice pick stuck
to the temple of a gambler who owed 10 pesos
in pusoy, a security guard ended by
swift slash of a cheated husband's bolo,
the top of his head hanging, sad lid
of a tin can, fodder for the sic o'clock news.

This body heaving under faded printed sheets,
hooked to a machine, furrowed forehead
of a familiar face. This tentacled body, flanked
by beeping sentries that sometimes malfunction,

This is not yours.

But are your gestures yours?
Shrug of shoulders, crease of brow,
shudder of tears, when I sing, when
your siblings are here, when we pray,
when my sister and I forgot you were
in the room and talked about that
time I was molested by someone you know.

Found in your dresser drawer, in cursive,
"My life support is only God Almighty
and His Son Jesus Christ and the Holy Spirit.
Never artificial respirator," written
posthaste in front of envelope with
"Open in Case of Death" scribbled
across seal, your familiar script,
many times forged for excuse slips,
fieldtrip forms; now here we are,
me, your reluctant signatory; and here
you are, unwitting accomplice to our
betrayal; breathing, but not on your own.

At 3:16, a message sent in frantic electronic squawking,
orange light flashing, a minute to let settle,

the sound of pandesal peddler horn forever defamed.

Another day, another 3:16, above
a text message from Ate to your daughter
not easily swayed, your faith excursion
companion; believer of lost mothers looking
for something to believe, receiver of unwanted faith
healing, dubious witness of transfigurations.
Do you remember? The Santo Nino's hands
embossed upon the sanctified swindler's?
You whispered, "Look, look. Upon her palms,
images of little Jesus's tiny hands?" And I
thought maybe I wasn't blessed to see, but
I pretended, exclaimed *"Oo nga."* Yes, I see!
I was nine years old.

These pedicured toes, still golden but
tumid, ripe with unwanted fluids; these
are not yours. This swollen knee, bearing
surgical scar; that time Tita Et warned you
through her clairvoyant cards to be careful,
watch your step, but you slipped on rain-slicked
driveway, broke your patella, typed your scripts
at the hospital for weeks, while your knee
healed, all the time exalting your friend's
psychic powers, saying you should have heeded.

Should we heed now? Is this you sending
3:16 messages? Are you now telepathic? Psychic?
Do you wish perhaps you that you did not cut off,
supernatural friends, sinning skeptics from
your born-again life? Do you wish I were less sinful?

Do you wish you were?

And now your fate lies not in God, not in Estrella,
not in your hand or your children's but in
a committee of suited men in white robes
that pray to a God not too different from yours.

Why is it that to play god is fine, but to honor
your wish is an affront to the Divine?

www.ingramcontent.com/pod-product-compliance
Lightning Source LLC
LaVergne TN
LVHW041553070426
835507LV00011B/1075